I0459172

The Enlightened Believer

EMMANUEL ADEWUSI

CCCG Publishing House

THE ENLIGHTENED BELIEVER

Author: Emmanuel Adewusi

ISBN: 978-1-989099-48-3 (hardcover)

ISBN: 978-1-989099-49-0 (ebook)

First Printing 2025

Contents

Dedication

I am eternally grateful to the team God has personally assembled to ensure that the written messages He has given to me are made available to the world.

To my wife, Pastor Ibukun Adewusi, thank you for holding the forte while I spent countless hours writing this book. You are truly a divine helper. I love you.

To my counsellor, friend, teacher, enlightener, the Holy Spirit, I am blessed to have you on my side. With you, I am guaranteed to live the life that Jesus Christ died on the cross for me to live.

1

You Must Be Enlightened

"In the beginning was the Word, and the Word was with God, and the Word was God. He was in the beginning with God. All things were made through Him, and without Him nothing was made that was made. In Him was life, and the life was the light of men. And the light shines in the darkness, and the darkness did not comprehend it." (John 1:1-5)

Enlightenment means to be full of light. It means to be illuminated. It means to be aware and to understand. It means your eyes are open to the truth, and you can see. It means to know the truth. Knowledge is not the same as enlightenment. A person can acquire knowledge but not understand the acquired knowledge. Enlightenment is a step higher than knowledge acquisition. When you know, you will effectively apply your knowledge where necessary.

The concepts expressed in this book differ from those of other religions. They might espouse similar terminologies, just as I have, but they propose different means of enlightenment. The concepts might appear familiar but are worlds apart in numerous ways. I will endeavour to provide biblical references that guide us on the right path.

WHY YOU SHOULD PAY THE PRICE TO BE ENLIGHTENED

There are many reasons why believers must seek to be enlightened. We must strive to increase the intensity of the light we operate in. Proverbs 4:18 says that the path of the just grows brighter and brighter until the most perfect day.

To Lead Unbelievers to Jesus

Without the children of God showing unbelievers the way, they cannot find God. We are the light of the world to show unbelievers the way back to God. We are to lift up a banner for the people of God. The god of this world

(Satan) has blinded the eyes of unbelievers, but the power in the light of God within us can show them the way back to God through Jesus Christ.

"For so the Lord has commanded us "I have set you as a light to the Gentiles, That you should be for salvation to the ends of the earth." (Acts 13:47)

Until your light starts shining, unbelievers cannot return to their loving Heavenly Father.

Command Over Spiritual Forces

To be enlightened is to be in command. The kingdom of God is often called the kingdom of light, while the kingdom of Satan is often called the kingdom of darkness.

"To open their eyes, in order to turn them from darkness to light, and from the power of Satan to God, that they may receive forgiveness of sins and an inheritance among those who are sanctified by faith in Me." (Acts 26:18)

A believer can be delivered from the dominion of darkness but still be exposed to the enemy's attacks and power. Colossians 1:13 states, *"He has delivered us from the power of darkness and conveyed us into the kingdom of the Son of His love."* Remember, Jesus said that a demon can be cast out of a person, but it could still come back under certain conditions.

"When an unclean spirit goes out of a man, he goes through dry places, seeking rest, and finds none. Then he says, 'I will return to my house from which I came.' And when he comes, he finds it empty, swept, and put in order. Then he goes and takes with him seven other spirits more wicked than himself, and they enter and dwell there; and the last state of that man is worse than the first. So shall it also be with this wicked generation." (Matthew 12:43-45)

Did you notice that the demonic spirits did not face any opposition from the man when they wanted to come back? They simply returned because the house was empty, swept and put in order, but it was not filled with light. A person can be delivered, but if they are not enlightened, they can be attacked again by the enemy as many times as possible and even bring some demon friends along. That will not be your portion in Jesus' name (Amen).

Light is the only permanent defence against onslaughts from the kingdom of darkness.

Enlightenment occurs in every aspect of human life. There is spiritual enlightenment and mental enlighten-ment. Spiritual enlightenment happens when we connect with God through Jesus Christ. Mental enlightenment occurs when we understand something; this is that aha moment we experience when we finally grasp a subject.

Divine Direction

Without the light of God, it would be impossible to find our way to heaven while travelling through the earth. That is why David exclaimed, *"Your word is a lamp unto my feet and a light unto my path"* (Psalms 119:105). Are you going anywhere worth going? If you arc, the light of God is what you need for direction.

We cannot find our way and get the answers we need in a world full of voices without light. When the children of Israel left Egypt for the promised land, the Bible says God directed them. He did this using the pillar of cloud by day and the pillar of fire by night. This is found in Exodus 13:21-22, *"And the LORD went before them by day in a pillar of cloud to lead the way, and by night in a pillar of fire to give them light, so as to go by day and night. He did not take away the pillar of cloud by day or the pillar of fire by night from before the people."*

God is still doing the same for His children today. God is still going before us in a pillar of cloud by day and a pillar of fire by night. God's approach can change, but His purpose never changes. He is no respecter of persons. If He did it for the Israelites, He wants to do the same for us. Shout Hallelujah!

2

To Be Known Spiritually

*"And the evil spirit answered and said, "Jesus
I know, and Paul I know; but who are you?"*
(Acts 19:15)

The principal way that people are known in the spiritual
realm is by the light in them or upon them. In Acts 19:15,
the demon acknowledged that it knew Jesus and Paul. This
was mainly because of the light they carried. The seven
sons of Sceva did not carry the light of God; hence, they
were not known by the demonic forces.

An enlightened person knows and is made known by the
light they carry.

From Scriptures, we understand that the whole world lies under the sway of the devil —in darkness (1 John 5:19). This is not difficult to believe if you look to see all the negative things happening around you. Those of us that are walking with Jesus are in the light.

"Then Jesus spoke to them again, saying, "I am the light of the world. He who follows Me shall not walk in darkness, but have the light of life."(John 8:12)

When there is darkness all around, and you see a flicker of light, I am sure that will get your attention. The spirit of those who believe in Jesus Christ as the Son of God immediately lights up. This light shines brighter as we grow in our faith and knowledge of God through Jesus Christ.

Access to Your Spiritual Inheritance

All good things in this world are hidden. It takes access to light to find them.

When we are enlightened, we begin to see what God has in store for us. We begin to see that we are born winners and not losers. We begin to see that we are not victims of life but joint architects with God. We begin to see that once we agree with God's master plan for our lives and obey His instructions, no evil force can hinder our success.

Ignorance is Dangerous

Jesus was reported to have only wept twice. One was a demonstration of his love for Lazarus (John 11:35), and the other was a result of the ignorance of the people of Israel (Luke 19:41-42).

The Bible tells us that people perish for lack of knowledge. People are destroyed for lack of understanding. In Job 26:12, we are told, *"but if they do not obey, they shall perish by the sword, and they shall die without knowledge."* It is also noted in Proverbs 5:23 that *"He shall die for lack of instruction, and in the greatness of his folly he shall go astray."* The Bible goes further in Hosea 4:6, saying, *"my people are destroyed for lack of knowledge. Because you have rejected knowledge, I also will reject you from being priest for Me; because you have forgotten the law of your God, I also will forget your children."*

Not being enlightened is the same as being ignorant. It is looking but not seeing. It is hearing but not listening. The Bible sounds the alarm against ignorance in Isaiah 42:18-20 saying, *"hear, you deaf; and look, you blind, that you may see. Who is blind but My servant, or deaf as My messenger whom I send? Who is blind as he who is perfect,*

And blind as the Lord's servant? Seeing many things, but you do not observe; Opening the ears, but he does not hear."

An Enlightened Believer is Stable/Confident/Strong/Obedient/Determined

Enlightenment and understanding refer to the same concept. The more you understand, the more enlightened you are, and vice versa.

Understanding comes from two words. They are "under" and "stand". This means you have a foundation. It has been said that you will fall for everything if you stand for nothing. Enlightenment gives you things to stand on.

Enlightenment provides a fortress for a believer. You are not afraid of anything or anyone.

Enlightenment provides strength. Light always has the strength to defeat darkness.

Understanding leads to enlightenment, which makes obedience easier. Many Christians find it difficult to obey God because they do not understand His instructions. It is difficult to disobey instructions that you know. If you do not obey an instruction, you most likely don't "fully" understand why you are supposed to do so.

Enlightened believers are resolute. It is hard to give up when enlightened about a particular aspect of life.

3

God is Light

"For You will light my lamp; The LORD my God will enlighten my darkness." (Psalms 18:28)

If enlightenment is defined as being full of light, the next logical question is, *"What is light?"*

Light is anything that brings illumination to a place, person or event. Light is the only thing that can dispel/eliminate darkness. Ephesians 5:13 specifically states *"but all things that are exposed are made manifest by the light, for whatever makes manifest is light."*

According to the Bible, God is light. The nature of God is expressed in three different forms: **God the Father, God the Son (the Living Word)** and **God the Holy Spirit.**

GOD THE FATHER

God the Father dwells in light

God the Father dwells in light, which is unapproachable, except God gives man access.

"Who alone has immortality, dwelling in unapproachable light, whom no man has seen or can see, to whom be honor and everlasting power. Amen." (1 Timothy 6:16)

"He reveals deep and secret things; He knows what is in the darkness, And light dwells with Him." (Daniel 2:22)

God the Father wraps Himself in light

The way we wear clothes as human beings is how God wears light as a garment.

"Bless the LORD, O my soul! O LORD my God, You are very great: You are clothed with honor and majesty, Who cover Yourself with light as with a garment, Who stretch out the heavens like a curtain." (Psalms 104:1-2)

God the Father is Light

Imagine the sun's intensity at noonday, and then imagine the light emanating from God.

"This is the message which we have heard from Him and declare to you, that God is light and in Him is no darkness at all. If we say that we have fellowship with Him, and walk in darkness, we lie and do not practice the truth. But if we walk in the light as He is in the light, we have fellowship with one another, and the blood of Jesus Christ His Son cleanses us from all sin." (1 John 1:5-7)

In the earthly realm, we know that light has different intensity levels. The intensity of God's light, however, is without comparison. The light from God's presence illuminates the heavens; there is no sun or moon to give light in heaven. You can only give what you have. God is light, and His light can illuminate the whole earth.

There shall be no night there: They need no lamp nor light of the sun, for the Lord God gives them light. And they shall reign forever and ever. (Revelation 22:5)

Any exposure to God is an exposure to light. Every time God reveals Himself to a person, they become enlightened. An example is the story of the change in Moses' facial appearance after spending time with God on the mountain. The Biblical account in Exodus 34:29-35 describes the event.

"Now it was so, when Moses came down from Mount Sinai (and the two tablets of the Testimony were in Moses' hand when he came down from the mountain), that Moses did not know that the skin of his face shone while he talked with Him. So when Aaron and all the children of Israel saw Moses, behold, the skin of his face shone, and they were afraid to come near him. Then Moses called to them, and Aaron and all the rulers of the congregation returned to him; and Moses talked with them. Afterward all the children of Israel came near, and he gave them as commandments all that the LORD had spoken with him on Mount Sinai. And when Moses had finished speaking with them, he put a veil on his face. But whenever Moses went in before the LORD to speak with Him, he would take the veil off until he came out; and he would come out and speak to the children of Israel whatever he had been commanded. And whenever the children of Israel saw the face of Moses, that the skin of Moses' face shone, then Moses would put the veil on his face again, until he went in to speak with Him."

Every genuine positive encounter with God will bring about enlightenment. God's nature will rub off on you.

GOD THE SON

God the Son is light. His light is shown all through Scriptures in different ways.

A Great Light

"The people who sat in darkness have seen a great light, And upon those who sat in the region and shadow of death Light has dawned." (Matthew 4:16)

The Light of the World

"Then Jesus spoke to them again, saying, "I am the light of the world. He who follows Me shall not walk in darkness, but have the light of life." (John 8:12)

The Giver of Light

You can only give what you have. According to the Bible, Jesus Christ gives light to those who are willing (Ephesians 5:14). The moment a person becomes born again, they are given light by Jesus Christ. John the Baptist bore witness to Jesus being the Light. John 1:6-9 recounts that *"There was a man sent from God, whose name was John. This man came for a witness, to bear witness of the Light, that all through him might believe. He was not that Light, but was sent to bear witness of that Light. That was the true Light which gives light to every man coming into the world."*

God the Holy Spirit

God the Holy Spirit is light. According to Ephesians 5:13, anything that exposes hidden things is light. The Holy Spirit is the illuminator. The Holy Spirit exposes hidden things so that we can understand the Word of God.

Bible teachers use the word illumination to describe the work of the Holy Spirit, which enables us to understand and apply the spiritual message of the Scriptures. When Jesus met two disciples on the road to Emmaus, *"He expounded to them in all the Scriptures the things concerning Himself."* (Luke 24:27) *Later, "their eyes were opened, and they knew Him"* (Luke 24:31). In illumination, the Holy Spirit opens our eyes so that we may know the Scriptures.

Illumination is a ministry of the Holy Spirit, who is given *"that we might know the things that are freely given to us of God"* (1 Corinthians 2:12). When the Holy Spirit does this work in our life, it results in our gaining a complete understanding of the Scriptures (John 16:13-15; 1 Corinthians

2:12-16). The illuminating work of the Holy Spirit depends on our relationship with God.

We cannot understand the Scriptures apart from the Holy Spirit's work of illumination. Our spiritual eyes are blind, so we cannot see the things of God.

Light is to the spirit and soul, what food is to the body. Just as the body needs food to thrive, the spirit and soul of man need light to thrive. God is the giver of that illumination that every spirit and soul needs to thrive.

4

The Believer is Light

"The dominion of light over darkness is instant and unquestionable." ——Dr. David Oyedepo

Everyone who genuinely believes in Jesus Christ is light. The intensity of that light increases or decreases in the course of a believer's lifetime, based on their devotion to Jesus Christ. Jesus said His disciples are the light of the world (Matthew 5:14). It is difficult to conceal light; one way or another, it finds a way to shine.

Believers have been set as a light to unbelievers in the world, bringing them to salvation.

"For so the Lord has commanded us: 'I have set you as a light to the Gentiles, That you should be for salvation to the ends of the earth." (Acts 13:47)

The believer is told they are the light, while an unbeliever is the darkness. Light has no communion with darkness as Christ has no accord with Belial (the devil). This is validated in 2 Corinthians 6:14-15, *"Do not be unequally yoked together with unbelievers. For what fellowship has righteousness with lawlessness? And what communion has light with darkness? And what accord has Christ with Belial? Or what part has a believer with an unbeliever?"*

Even though believers are light, we can decide not to shine. Our actions or inactions can cause us to fail to shine. Our Lord and Saviour, Jesus Christ, charged us to let our light shine. I decree in Jesus' name; your light will shine for the world to see.

"Nor do they light a lamp and put it under a basket, but on a lampstand, and it gives light to all who are in the house. Let your light so shine before men, that they may see your good works and glorify your Father in heaven." (Matthew 5:15-16)

The world we live in is covered in darkness. We are in a time and season when light is needed more than ever. This is the time when believers are expected to shine more than ever before. The enlightened believer is expected to roll back the dominion of darkness in all their areas of influence.

Many homes are being covered in darkness. Schools are espousing perverse and destructive ideologies. Governments are implementing devilish agendas that are destroying the sound moral fabric of their nations. The Biblical prophecy of what the last days will look like is already being fulfilled at an alarming rate. We are in a time when narcissistic people are gladly being elected as presidents of nations. It is a time when corporations are amassing wealth at an egregious rate. A time when decisions are being made at different leadership quarters that are dragging more people into dire poverty. Love for pleasure is increasing exponentially. In fact, pleasures have become the sole motive for work, among many. What is most shocking is that these things are happening worldwide—Asia, the Americas, Africa, Europe etc. The amplified bible (AMP) renders 2 Timothy 3:1-5 thus:

"But understand this, that in the last days dangerous times [of great stress and trouble] will come [difficult days that will be hard to bear]. For people will be lovers of self [narcissistic, self-focused], lovers of money [impelled by greed], boastful, arrogant, revilers, disobedient to parents, ungrate-

ful, unholy and profane, [and they will be] unloving [devoid of natural human affection, calloused and inhumane], irreconcilable, malicious gossips, devoid of self-control [intemperate, immoral], brutal, haters of good, traitors, reckless, conceited, lovers of [sensual] pleasure rather than lovers of God, holding to a form of [outward] godliness (religion), although they have denied its power [for their conduct nullifies their claim of faith]. Avoid such people and keep far away from them."

A believer is first enlightened before being expected to illuminate every area under their control with the light of Jesus Christ.

"Do everything without murmuring or questioning [the providence of God], so that you may prove yourselves to be blameless and guileless, innocent and uncontaminated, children of God without blemish in the midst of a [morally] crooked and [spiritually] perverted generation, among whom you are seen as bright lights [beacons shining out clearly] in the world [of darkness]." (Philippians 2:14-15, AMP)

The light of God in believers will lead unbelievers back to God. In the last days, unbelievers will use the light they see in believers as crumbs, to find their way back to our loving, merciful Heavenly Father.

5

Steps to Enlightenment

"Oh, send out Your light and Your truth! Let them lead me; Let them bring me to Your holy hill and to Your tabernacle." (Psalms 43:3)

God is wrapped in pure light (Psalms 104:2). Enlightenment comes when you genuinely contact God. The more time you spend with God, the more enlightened you become. It's impossible to jump into a pool of water and not get wet. It is impossible to connect with God and not get enlightened genuinely.

Enlightenment is not a one-time event. The Bible tells us, *"but the path of the just is like the shining sun, that shines ever brighter unto the perfect day"* (Proverbs 4:18). It is dangerous to be exposed to the entirety of God's light suddenly. Have you ever experienced what it felt like when someone suddenly turned on a bright light after you woke up? I'm sure you briskly closed your eyes and gradually opened them again. When you are suddenly exposed to bright light, it can damage your physical eyes. This also applies to your understanding of spiritual things.

When an individual or group is suddenly exposed to bright light after being in darkness, they typically reject the light for some time. This is natural. They need time to adjust to the bright light they were exposed to. This is why enlightenment will come with persecution. In Mark 5:17, Jesus was begged to leave Decapolis because they were in gross darkness, and the light Jesus carried was too bright for them. After some years, they welcomed Jesus back to their town because the man who was previously mad had been preaching about Jesus Christ to them (Mark 7:31-37).

Every provision in the kingdom of God has well-defined steps for its attainment. If the steps are not clearly defined in Scriptures, you have every right to doubt its scriptural veracity.

As Christians, we must take steps to be enlightened. In addition to being born again, we must continually take other steps to increase the intensity of the light we carry.

The primary motive while following these steps must be LOVE. Any motive other than love will take you to the wrong destination. The Bible tells us that through love, we can be on this earth as Jesus is in heaven (1 John 4:17).

You Must Be Born Again

Accepting Jesus as your Lord and Saviour is the first step to accessing the goodies of the kingdom of God. You cannot see the kingdom of God without being born again.

Jesus replied, "Very truly I tell you, no one can see the kingdom of God unless they are born again." (John 3:3)

Whenever you see the word "understanding" in the Bible, you can safely replace it with enlightenment. Jesus has come to enlighten us so we don't remain in darkness, void of understanding.

We know also that the Son of God has come and has given us understanding, so that we may know him who is true. And we are in him who is true by being in his Son Jesus Christ. He is the true God and eternal life. (1 John 5:20)

Jesus said, *"I have come as a light into the world, that whoever believes in Me should not abide in darkness"* (John 12:46). Believing in Jesus is the first step out of darkness.

The Holy Spirit grants us access to the kingdom of God. The kingdom of God is not a place but wherever the Spirit of God is. Anywhere the Holy Spirit is, the kingdom of God is present (Luke 10:8-12).

No one can receive the Holy Spirit without being washed in the precious blood of Jesus Christ. No one can receive the Holy Spirit without accepting Jesus as their Lord and Savior. No matter how long you have been attending church or even reading the Bible, if you have never accepted Jesus into your heart, you are not born again. You are not yet born again if you have never confessed that Jesus is Lord.

With the heart, man believes, and with the mouth, confession is made unto salvation. To be saved or born again, you must believe and confess that Jesus is Lord and that God raised Him from the dead. If you only believe but never confess it, you are not saved. You are not saved if you admit it but do not believe it.

"But what does it say? "The word is near you, in your mouth and in your heart" (that is, the word of faith which we

preach): that if you confess with your mouth the Lord Jesus and believe in your heart that God has raised Him from the dead, you will be saved. For with the heart one believes unto righteousness, and with the mouth confession is made unto salvation. For the Scripture says, "Whoever believes on Him will not be put to shame." For there is no distinction between Jew and Greek, for the same Lord over all is rich to all who call upon Him. For "whoever calls on the name of the LORD shall be saved." (Romans 10:8-13)

During one of our Come and See services in 2016, I had an experience that validates this. A former classmate of mine was born a Muslim. During his schooling in Canada, he gained interest in learning about Jesus. He attended church services for about eight years. During those years, everyone kept telling him about Jesus but never invited him to make a decision—to believe and confess that Jesus is Lord. However, he believed that Jesus is Lord but never confessed it. During the Come and See service he attended, I invited anyone who wanted to acknowledge Jesus as Lord, and he honoured that invitation. He finally became born again that day, and his life transformed thereafter.

Now that you believe that Jesus is the Son of God, why don't you make that confession right away? Skip to the

Sinner's Prayer Section in this book right away and make the confession.

We are only saved when we confess Jesus Christ as Lord and Saviour. Salvation gives us access to the kingdom of heaven and opens the door to enlightenment. It is like getting a visa to visit a country. That is why the Bible says that until we believe in Jesus, we cannot "see" the kingdom of God. Salvation is the beginning of the journey. It is not the end in itself but the beginning.

Now that you are saved, you have access to the treasures in the kingdom of God, one of which is enlightenment (i.e. a primary treasure).

BE FILLED (BAPTIZED) WITH THE HOLY SPIRIT

You cannot gain access to light without the Holy Spirit. You cannot be enlightened without an encounter with the Holy Spirit.

Another definition of enlightenment is "to gain knowledge of the truth". There is the truth about the world we live in and the life afterwards. Compared with the lies out there, truth is miniscule. There are significantly more lies being disseminated than truth. The Holy Spirit is the agent that brings us to the knowledge of the truth in every area of life. This is why Jesus said *"I still have many things to say to you, but you cannot bear them now. However, when He, the Spirit of truth, has come, He will guide you into all truth; for He will not speak on His own authority, but whatever He hears He will speak; and He will tell you things to come."* (John 16:12-13)

For instance, the world will have you believe that some diseases are incurable. This, however, is a lie. Even doctors can mistakenly spread the lie that some diseases are incurable until they see a miracle take place. Jesus is the healer; if He could raise the dead, no disease is beyond His power to heal. If you are sick or in pain and you believe these words, I command you to be healed now, in Jesus' name! (Amen).

I came to the knowledge of the truth concerning healing a few years ago. This has enabled me to join the league of those who can boldly proclaim they can never be sick again. This was triggered by revelation from the Holy Spirit.

I came to the knowledge of the truth concerning prosperity a few years ago. This has also enabled me to join the league of those who can never be poor again. The Holy

Spirit is the carrier of divine secrets. Jesus said *"He will take of what is mine and declare it to you"* (John 16:14).

When you give your life to Jesus Christ and are filled with the Holy Spirit, it is not simply to speak in tongues. It is to fellowship with God through the Holy Spirit.

The Holy Spirit is our companion and guide. He wants to share secrets with us if we are willing to listen. The Holy Spirit is our access to the secrets and things of God.

There are secrets you will gain access to that will put you in command of financial resources, your health, your marriage, your family, etc. These secrets are not for those outside (i.e., the unbelievers) but for those who love God (i.e., the children of God). Hear what the Bible says about this in 1 Corinthians 2:6-14:

"However, we speak wisdom among those who are mature, yet not the wisdom of this age, nor of the rulers of this age, who are coming to nothing. But we speak the wisdom of God in a mystery, the hidden wisdom which God ordained before the ages for our glory, which none of the rulers of this age knew; for had they known, they would not have crucified the Lord of glory. But as it is written: "Eye has not seen, nor ear heard, Nor have entered into the heart of man The things which God has prepared for those who love Him."

But God has revealed them to us through His Spirit. For the Spirit searches all things, yes, the deep things of God. For what man knows the things of a man except the spirit of the man which is in him? Even so no one knows the things of God except the Spirit of God. Now we have received, not the spirit of the world, but the Spirit who is from God, that we might know the things that have been freely given to us by God. These things we also speak, not in words which man's wisdom teaches but which the Holy Spirit teaches, comparing spiritual things with spiritual. But the natural man does not receive the things of the Spirit of God, for they are foolishness to him; nor can he know them, because they are spiritually discerned."

The Holy Spirit is the conduit for transferring secrets from God the Father and God the Son to us (His children). The Holy Spirit makes those secrets known to our spirits. Our spirits, in turn, make them known to our minds so that we can put them to good use. Praise the Lord! Hallelujah!!!

Baptism in the Holy Spirit

Jesus introduced the Holy Spirit to His disciples in John 14:16-17: *"And I will ask the Father, and he will give you another advocate to help you and be with you forever— the Spirit of truth. The world cannot accept him because it nei-*

ther sees him nor knows him. But you know him, for he lives with you and will be in you."

On one occasion, he gave them this command in Acts 1:5: *"Do not leave Jerusalem, but wait for the gift my Father promised, which you have heard me speak about. For John baptized with water, but in a few days you will be baptized with the Holy Spirit."*

The promise was fulfilled when the Holy Spirit descended on the thirsty disciples, now Apostles, as they heeded Christ's instructions to tarry in Jerusalem until that promise was fulfilled.

"When the day of Pentecost came, they were all together in one place. Suddenly a sound like the blowing of a violent wind came from heaven and filled the whole house where they were sitting. They saw what seemed to be tongues of fire that separated and came to rest on each of them. All of them were filled with the Holy Spirit and began to speak in other tongues as the Spirit enabled them." (Acts 2:1-4)

Baptism simply means an immersion. Baptism in the Holy Spirit means being filled with the Holy Spirit. This should not be mistaken for being born again. We become born again when we accept that Jesus is Lord. However, from the account in Acts 10, we see that being baptized in the

Holy Spirit can happen simultaneously with being born again. We saw this happen in the story of Cornelius.

"There was a certain man in Caesarea called Cornelius, a centurion of what was called the Italian Regiment, a devout man and one who feared God with all his household, who gave alms generously to the people, and prayed to God always. About the ninth hour of the day, he saw clearly in a vision an angel of God coming in and saying to him, "Cornelius!" And when he observed him, he was afraid, and said, "What is it, lord?" So he said to him, "Your prayers and your alms have come up for a memorial before God. Now send men to Joppa, and send for Simon whose surname is Peter. He is lodging with Simon, a tanner, whose house is by the sea. He will tell you what you must do." (Acts 10:1-6)

Even though Cornelius was devout, he was not born again because he had not heard the gospel of Christ or had the chance to accept Jesus Christ into his heart. The Lord then sent an angel to ask Cornelius to send for Peter. Peter's mission was to preach the gospel to Cornelius and his household so they can believe in Jesus Christ.

"While Peter was still speaking these words, the Holy Spirit fell upon all those who heard the word. And those of the circumcision who believed were astonished, as many as came

with Peter, because the gift of the Holy Spirit had been poured out on the Gentiles also. For they heard them speak with tongues and magnify God." (Acts 10:44-46)

The word "heard" in verse 44 means that they received Peter's word concerning Jesus as the Christ. Once that happened, according to John 1:12, they became children of God, thereby, fulfilling the condition to receive the baptism of the Holy Spirit.

In many other instances in scriptures, including that of the disciples, they became born again before receiving the baptism of the Holy Spirit. This shows that the disciples had received Jesus as the Christ and Lord.

"Then, the same day at evening, being the first day of the week, when the doors were shut where the disciples were assembled, for fear of the Jews, Jesus came and stood in the midst, and said to them, 'Peace be with you.' When He had said this, He showed them His hands and His side. Then the disciples were glad when they saw the Lord. So Jesus said to them again, 'Peace to you! As the Father has sent Me, I also send you.' And when He had said this, He breathed on them, and said to them, 'Receive the Holy Spirit. If you forgive the sins of any, they are forgiven them; if you retain the sins of any, they are retained.'" (John 20:19-23)

Early Converts

Another example is of the early converts receiving Jesus as Lord and being subsequently baptized in the Holy Spirit

"Then Peter said to them, 'Repent, and let every one of you be baptized in the name of Jesus Christ for the remission of sins; and you shall receive the gift of the Holy Spirit. For the promise is to you and to your children, and to all who are afar off, as many as the Lord our God will call.' And with many other words he testified and exhorted them, saying, 'Be saved from this perverse generation.' Then those who gladly received his word were baptized; and that day about three thousand souls were added to them." (Acts 2:38-41)

The Samaritans

The Samaritans in Acts 8 are another example. Acts 8:4-6, shows the people in Samaria accepting Jesus as Lord:

"Therefore those who were scattered went everywhere preaching the word. Then Philip went down to the city of Samaria and preached Christ to them. And the multitudes with one accord heeded the things spoken by Philip, hearing and seeing the miracles which he did." (Acts 8:4-6)

Believers in Samaria

Subsequently, in Acts 8:14-17, it shows those believers in Samaria receiving the baptism of the Holy Spirit:

"Now when the apostles who were at Jerusalem heard that Samaria had received the word of God, they sent Peter and John to them, who, when they had come down, prayed for them that they might receive the Holy Spirit. For as yet He had fallen upon none of them. They had only been baptized in the name of the Lord Jesus. Then they laid hands on them, and they received the Holy Spirit." (Acts 8:14-17)

Paul

Paul received the Holy Spirit when Ananias laid hands on him.

"And Ananias went his way and entered the house; and laying his hands on him he said, 'Brother Saul, the Lord Jesus, who appeared to you on the road as you came, has sent me that you may receive your sight and be filled with the Holy Spirit.' Immediately there fell from his eyes something like scales, and he received his sight at once; and he arose and was baptized." (Acts 9:17-18)

Ways to Receive the Baptism of the Holy Spirit

By Waiting On The Lord In Prayer And Worship

The disciples waited for the baptism in the Holy Spirit by remaining in prayer.

"Then they returned to Jerusalem from the mount called Olivet, which is near Jerusalem, a Sabbath day's journey. And when they had entered, they went up into the upper room where they were staying: Peter, James, John, and Andrew; Philip and Thomas; Bartholomew and Matthew; James the son of Alphaeus and Simon the Zealot; and Judas the son of James. These all continued with one accord in prayer and supplication, with the women and Mary the mother of Jesus, and with His brothers" (Acts 1:12-14)

We then saw that the Holy Spirit came upon them in response to their prayers.

"When the Day of Pentecost had fully come, they were all with one accord in one place. And suddenly there came a sound from heaven, as of a rushing mighty wind, and it filled the whole house where they were sitting. Then there appeared to them divided tongues, as of fire, and one sat

upon each of them. And they were all filled with the Holy Spirit and began to speak with other tongues, as the Spirit gave them utterance" (Acts 2:1-4)

The disciples were again filled with the Holy Spirit after they prayed.

"After they prayed, the place where they were meeting was shaken. And they were all filled with the Holy Spirit and spoke the word of God boldly" (Acts 4:31)

You wait in prayer and worship by asking God to baptize you in the Holy Spirit. You can pray this prayer in faith:

Heavenly Father, I thank you that I am Your child. I thank You for always answering me whenever I call on You. You promised to give the Holy Spirit to those who ask. Right now, I ask You to baptize me in the Holy Spirit. Thank You, Father, for answering my prayer. In Jesus' name, Amen.

After praying this prayer in faith, begin to praise God and thank Him for the baptism in the Holy Spirit you have received. As you continue in this, I strongly believe that the Holy Spirit will come upon you.

By Laying on of Hands

The baptism in the Holy Spirit can be received through the laying on of hands of someone that is filled with the Holy Spirit. The disciples in Samaria received the Holy Spirit when Peter and John laid hands on them.

"Now when the apostles who were at Jerusalem heard that Samaria had received the word of God, they sent Peter and John to them, who, when they had come down, prayed for them that they might receive the Holy Spirit. For as yet He had fallen upon none of them. They had only been baptized in the name of the Lord Jesus. Then they laid hands on them, and they received the Holy Spirit" (Acts 8:14-17)

Paul received the Holy Spirit when Ananias laid hands on him.

"And Ananias went his way and entered the house; and laying his hands on him he said, 'Brother Saul, the Lord Jesus, who appeared to you on the road as you came, has sent me that you may receive your sight and be filled with the Holy Spirit.' Immediately there fell from his eyes something like scales, and he received his sight at once; and he arose and was baptized" (Acts 9:17-18)

By Listening to an Anointed Message

Cornelius and his household received the baptism in the Holy Spirit while Peter was preaching the gospel to them. Perhaps, God knew that this was the most effective way to demonstrate to the early church that He was calling the gentiles to be Christians as well.

"While Peter was still speaking these words, the Holy Spirit fell upon all those who heard the word" (Acts 10:44)

Evidence of the Baptism in the Holy Spirit

Speaking in Tongues

The examples referred to from scriptures clearly show that after the baptism in the Holy Spirit, the disciples of Christ spoke in other tongues. This is in fulfillment of Christ's words concerning this.

"He who believes in Me, as the Scripture has said, out of his heart will flow rivers of living water." But this He spoke concerning the Spirit, whom those believing in Him would receive; for the Holy Spirit was not yet given, because Jesus was not yet glorified." (John 7:38-39, NKJV)

These examples below show us that speaking in tongues is evidence of being baptized in the Holy Spirit.

- *"Then there appeared to them divided tongues, as of fire, and one sat upon each of them. And they were all filled with the Holy Spirit and began to speak with other tongues, as the Spirit gave them utterance"* (Acts 2:3-4)

- *"While Peter was still speaking these words, the Holy Spirit fell upon all those who heard the word. And those of the circumcision who believed were astonished, as many as came with Peter, because the gift of the Holy Spirit had been poured out on the Gentiles also. For they heard them speak with tongues and magnify God"* (Acts 10:44-46)

Demonstrating the Fruits of the Holy Spirit

From scriptures, we understand that there are virtues that accompany the baptism in the Holy Spirit.

"But the fruit of the Spirit is love, joy, peace, long-suffering, kindness, goodness, faithfulness, gentleness, self-control. Against such, there is no law" (Galatians 5:22-23)

A person who is genuinely baptized in the Holy Spirit will display these virtues in increasing dimensions.

In addition to speaking in tongues and displaying the fruits of the Holy Spirit, the more we walk in the Spirit, the more we will manifest the gifts of the Holy Spirit in supernatural signs and wonders in increasing dimensions.

Remaining Filled with the Holy Spirit

The presence of the Holy Spirit in us is a gift from God (see Luke 11:13, NKJV). You must understand that the gift of the Holy Spirit can be lost. After being filled with the Holy Spirit, there are certain things to watch out for, in order to remain filled.

Avoid Sin

The Holy Spirit can be grieved by persisting in a sinful lifestyle or habit even after convictions from the Holy Spirit. There are many Christians who once knew what it meant to be filled with the Holy Spirit, but because of sin, have since gone astray.

"And do not grieve the Holy Spirit of God, by whom you were sealed for the day of redemption," (Ephesians 4:30, NKJV)

King David acknowledged the possibility of the presence of the Holy Spirit departing from a person in his prayer of repentance after he sinned by committing adultery with Bathsheba and arranging for her husband, Uriah, to be killed in battle.

"Do not cast me away from Your presence, And do not take Your Holy Spirit from me." (Psalms 51:11, NKJV)

Fellowship

The Holy Spirit's presence in us is not to be left dormant. We are to fellowship with Him regularly. We are to have the same kind of relationship that the Apostles had with Jesus Christ while He was on the earth.

"The grace of the Lord Jesus Christ, and the love of God, and the communion of the Holy Spirit be with you all. Amen." (2 Corinthians 13:14, NKJV)

Fellowship with the Holy Spirit can be as simple as asking Him questions. Engage with Him as you would a dear friend. Speak to Him, ask Him those burning questions that you have, pour out your heart to Him, cry and lean on Him when you are confused, and believe in faith that He is there listening. You can also regularly fellowship with Him by praying in the spirit (i.e., praying in your heavenly language). Jesus expressed His confidence in the presence of the Holy Spirit in Him in a profound statement that He made while under persecution.

"And He who sent Me is with Me. The Father has not left Me alone, for I always do those things that please Him." (John 8:29, NKJV)

Based on Christ's statement here, we see that His confidence in God's ever-abiding presence is based on Him being in right standing with God at all times. Being in right standing with God simply means being righteous. This does not mean that you do not make mistakes. It simply means that deliberate efforts are being made by you to live a life that pleases God, and when you are convicted of sin, you repent immediately.

With this confidence, begin to engage the Holy Spirit all through your day and watch as your relationship with Him deepens.

Do you know that as a child of God, you ought not to be afraid of demonic forces? Do you know that no weapon formed against you can prosper? Do you know that the devil is scared of you? Do you know that you are seated far above principalities and powers in heavenly places? These and many more truths that God can bring to your understanding if you ask Him to enlighten you.

PRAY TO BE ENLIGHTENED

We can become enlightened through prayer. Let me mention that prayer to God for enlightenment without being born again or baptized in the Holy Spirit will not be answered. Both are key prerequisites for the prayer for enlightenment to be effective.

Remember that I mentioned earlier that being enlightened also means understanding. It means having your eyes open and knowing the truth. One major hindrance in our quest to be enlightened is the active blindfolding weapon that the god of this world unleashed against the world. This weapon aims to make people see and hear but not understand.

"But even if our gospel is veiled, it is veiled to those who are perishing, whose minds the god of this age has blinded, who do not believe, lest the light of the gospel of the glory of Christ, who is the image of God, should shine on them. For we do not preach ourselves, but Christ Jesus the Lord, and ourselves your bondservants for Jesus' sake." (2 Corinthians 4:3-5)

With prayer and fasting, you can break the force of darkness hindering your ability to understand spiritual truths. Why do you get angry when you hear messages about giving? Why are you angry when you listen to messages about living a holy life? Why do you get angry when certain messages are preached from the same Holy Bible that we believe to be the word of God? It is because of the blindfolding weapon of the devil.

After you have prayed and nothing happened, add fasting to it. Remember that Jesus said, *"this kind can come out by nothing but prayer and fasting"* (Mark 9:29). As a child of God, you have a covenant right to understand the things of God. You have a right to the secrets of the kingdom of heaven. Keep praying until there is no hindrance to your understanding of spiritual things. Whenever you read the Word of God, you are meant to get insight from it. Whenever you listen to an anointed preaching or teaching of the Word of God, you are meant to get insight from it. Whenever you go through situations, you are meant to get insight from it. Do not stop until you have full, unhindered, unfettered access to the secrets of the kingdom of God.

In Isaiah 58:5-11, God was teaching the children of Israel about fasting. He was correcting some of the misconceptions they had about fasting. The main essence of fasting is not to provide an opportunity for you to suffer. It is not a competition in how much you can suffer or how long you can suffer. It is not your way of punishing yourself to get God's attention. Among other things, fasting makes your light break forth. Fasting causes God's light to break through you, destroying the hold of darkness in and around you.

There was a time when my wife complained to me that she could not understand Kenneth Copeland whenever he preached. This did not sound normal to me. I knew that the problem was not his accent. She could understand other people with the Southern United States accent, but why not Kenneth Copeland. We prayed together, and I commanded every blindfolding weapon of the devil, hindering her from understanding the word of God, to be removed and destroyed. Immediately, she began to understand Kenneth Copeland clearly and learned a great deal from his ministry.

In response to Daniel's prayer in Daniel 9, an angel was sent to give him the skill to understand. In other words, Daniel was enlightened about the topic he sought understanding of.

"Now while I was speaking, praying, and confessing my sin and the sin of my people Israel, and presenting my supplication before the LORD my God for the holy mountain of my God, yes, while I was speaking in prayer, the man Gabriel, whom I had seen in the vision at the beginning, being caused to fly swiftly, reached me about the time of the evening offering. And he informed me, and talked with me, and said, "O Daniel, I have now come forth to give you skill to understand. At the beginning of your supplications the command went out, and I have come to tell you, for you are greatly beloved; therefore consider the matter, and understand the vision." (Daniel 9:20-23)

In your prayers, ask God for the ability to understand things. Ask your heavenly Father for the skill to understand yourself, people, past and future events. Remember, it is written in Luke 24:45, *"He opened their understanding, that they might comprehend the Scriptures."* It is your covenant right to understand things, but until you ask, you will not receive. Until you seek, you will not find. Until you knock, the door will not open unto you (Matthew 7:7).

Apostle Paul prayed for the Church in Ephesus to be enlightened. He prayed for them to understand spiritual truth, which would grant them access to the necessary revelations to be in command. Apostle Paul prayed in Ephesians 1:17-21,

"That the God of our Lord Jesus Christ, the Father of glory, may give to you the spirit of wisdom and revelation in the knowledge of Him, the eyes of your understanding being enlightened; that you may know what is the hope of His calling, what are the riches of the glory of His inheritance in the saints, and what is the exceeding greatness of His power toward us who believe, according to the working of His mighty power which He worked in Christ when He raised Him from the dead and seated Him at His right hand in the heavenly places, far above all principality and power and might and dominion, and every name that is named, not only in this age but also in that which is to come."

David prayed that God would open his eyes to see wondrous things from the word of God. Pray this prayer from the depth of your heart,

"Heavenly Father, from today, may my eyes be open to myself, people and events the way you see them in Jesus' name, Amen."

Ezra prayed that God would enlighten their eyes (Ezra 9:8). Many people go through the same challenges repeatedly, without learning from the event. This is a sign that their eyes have been blinded. Many people get involved in the wrong relationships and repeat the same mistake repeatedly. You would think they would have realized their mistake, but they keep falling into the same trap. Sometimes, it simply means that their eyes are not open. If you fall into a trap without realizing why, chances are that you will fall into the same trap again and again.

"At the evening sacrifice I arose from my fasting; and having torn my garment and my robe, I fell on my knees and spread out my hands to the LORD my God. And I said: "O my God, I am too ashamed and humiliated to lift up my face to You, my God; for our iniquities have risen higher than our heads, and our guilt has grown up to the heavens. Since the days of our fathers to this day we have been very guilty, and for our iniquities we, our kings, and our priests have been delivered into the hand of the kings of the lands, to the sword, to captivity, to plunder, and to humiliation, as it is this day. And now for a little while grace has been shown from the LORD our God, to leave us a remnant to escape, and to give us a peg in His holy place, that our God may enlighten our eyes and give us a measure of revival in our bondage." (Ezra 9:5-8)

PURITY/HOLINESS

Purity is a state of heart that is right with God. It is a state where God has nothing bad against you, and the devil cannot find anything to use against you. Jesus described it clearly when He said, *"I will no longer talk much with you, for the ruler of this world is coming, and he has nothing in Me"* (John 14:30). Purity is being in a state where the devil has no accusation against you. Not necessarily because you never sinned but because you repented of every convicted sin immediately after you were convicted by the Holy Spirit.

Purity is being in a state where even the good things you do are from the right motive. It is a state of complete and total obedience to God.

It is only the pure in heart that can truly be enlightened. When you become born again and filled with the Holy Spirit, the amount of light you receive and display depends on the material your heart is made up of.

"To the pure all things are pure, but to those who are defiled and unbelieving nothing is pure; but even their mind and conscience are defiled. They profess to know God, but in

works they deny Him, being abominable, disobedient, and disqualified for every good work." (Titus 1:15-16)

If your heart is not right before God, you will never be able to understand spiritual things fully. Light has different effects depending on the material it is interacting with. In the same way, revelation from God has different effects depending on the type of heart that is receiving it.

There are three different categories of materials, and they are classified based on how they respond to light. I will use this classification of materials to describe the different types of hearts a person can have.

Transparent Conscience

This category of hearts allows every light it receives to settle and be reflected. These kinds of hearts let you see the light in its entirety. This is the state that God wants our hearts to always be in. Because God is holy, only those with pure hearts can "see" Him (Matthew 5:8).

"Then Paul, looking earnestly at the council, said, "Men and brethren, I have lived in all good conscience before God until this day." (Acts 23:1)

"Holding the mystery of the faith with a pure conscience." (1 Timothy 3:9)

"Let us draw near with a true heart in full assurance of faith, having our hearts sprinkled from an evil conscience and our bodies washed with pure water." (Hebrews 10:22)

"But the hour is coming, and now is, when the true worshipers will worship the Father in spirit and truth; for the Father is seeking such to worship Him." (John 4:23)

Opaque Conscience

This category of hearts blocks every light from going through. This is the state that all unbelievers are in. The god of this world, Satan, has blinded their hearts, so they are unable to accept, much less reflect the light of God.

"To the pure all things are pure, but to those who are defiled and unbelieving nothing is pure; but even their mind and conscience are defiled." (Titus 1:15)

Translucent Conscience

This category of hearts allows some light to pass through but restricts the remaining light from coming through.

They are selective in deciding which light comes through and which doesn't.

They are what I call double-dippers. They are sometimes neither here nor there. The Bible says that God would rather we be hot or cold but never lukewarm.

I know your works, that you are neither cold nor hot. I could wish you were cold or hot. So then, because you are lukewarm, and neither cold nor hot, I will vomit you out of My mouth. (Revelation 3:15-16)

Speaking lies in hypocrisy, having their own conscience seared with a hot iron. (1 Timothy 4:2)

Translucent hearts are conniving. They are deceiving and manipulating. They are neither lying nor telling the truth, and they are simply prevaricators. They try as much as possible to sit on the fence on key issues in an attempt not to hurt anyone. They are evasive. Most of the time, you don't know where they stand on issues. They shift their principles based on which external or internal voice is the loudest. They are those that bring the name of God to disrepute because of their double life. Those on the outside look at them thinking they are examples of Christ but get disappointed because they are not.

Purity of heart or conscience is a prerequisite for being enlightened and remaining enlightened. Without purity, we cannot see God. Our connection with God is what guarantees enlightenment. When you are pure, the King of kings will be your friend (Proverbs 22:11).

Daily Soak in the Presence of God

God is the father of lights (James 1:17). The more time you sincerely spend in His presence, the more enlightened you will become. The light in God's presence will rub off on you.

Moses had an encounter with God that made his face shine. He spent forty days and forty nights in the presence of God. He wanted and desired to be in the presence of God. He was not forced to be there. He craved the presence of God, and he was rewarded. It is impossible to sincerely spend time in God's presence without tangible proof. The example of Moses is a literal case of enlightenment.

"Then the LORD said to Moses, "Write these words, for according to the tenor of these words I have made a covenant with you and with Israel." So he was there with the LORD forty days and forty nights; he neither ate bread nor drank water. And He wrote on the tablets the words of the covenant,

the Ten Commandments. Now it was so, when Moses came down from Mount Sinai (and the two tablets of the Testimony were in Moses' hand when he came down from the mountain), that Moses did not know that the skin of his face shone while he talked with Him. So when Aaron and all the children of Israel saw Moses, behold, the skin of his face shone, and they were afraid to come near him." (Exodus 34:27-30)

You might be wondering, how can I spend forty days and forty nights in the presence of God? You don't necessarily have to spend that long to connect with God. The Bible records another example of Jesus having a similar experience. This happened on what we call the mountain of transfiguration. Jesus did not spend forty days and forty nights like Moses did before even clothes reflected the light of God.

"Now after six days Jesus took Peter, James, and John, and led them up on a high mountain apart by themselves; and He was transfigured before them. His clothes became shining, exceedingly white, like snow, such as no launderer on earth can whiten them. And Elijah appeared to them with Moses, and they were talking with Jesus." (Mark 9:2-4)

"And when He came to the disciples, He saw a great multitude around them, and scribes disputing with them. Immediately, when they saw Him, all the people were greatly amazed, and running to Him, greeted Him." (Mark 9:14-15)

When you become enlightened, people will begin to be amazed by the happenings in your life. You will no longer be looked down upon. Instead, you will be looked up to in amazement. The price to pay is worth it.

To make your time with God worthwhile and experience this deeper dimension of His presence, your soul must hunger and thirst for God the way a deer pants for water. Psalms 42:1-2 declares, *"As the deer pants for the water brooks, So pants my soul for You, O God. My soul thirsts for God, for the living God. When shall I come and appear before God?"*

Intimacy with God is found only in the realm of the spirit. Spiritually, your process of discovering a deeper dimension of God's presence involves longing, thirsting, and seeking. David wrote, *"O God, You are my God; Early will I seek You; My soul thirsts for You; My flesh longs for You In a dry and thirsty land Where there is no water. So I have looked*

for You in the sanctuary, To see Your power and Your glory."
(Psalms 63:1-2)

Intimacy with God is found only in the realm of the spirit. There is a place of deep anointing, deep presence, and deep intimacy with God Almighty, where *deep calls unto deep* or *spirit calls unto spirit*. It is a place so pure that the presence of Almighty God consumes every part of your being; a deep place where there is perfect communion between your spirit and every dimension of God's presence. Your soul is stirred, and there is a breakthrough in the spirit (Psalms 42:7). In this kind of intimacy, you will gain access to enlightenment in God.

If you dare seek God this way regularly, your light will never be lost. You will always be evergreen. Your strength will continually be renewed as the eagles (Isaiah 40:31), and it will seem like you never lose an iota of the presence of God.

Search for Pure Light

"The lamp of the body is the eye. If therefore your eye is good, your whole body will be full of light." (Matthew 6:22)

You must have a question you desperately need answers to. It is that question and the desperation with which we search that will open up the light we need.

You can become enlightened by searching for light. Remember that enlightened simply means to be full of light. The more "lighted" you are, the more enlightened you become. You can have light in some areas and not have it in other areas. It is possible to be in command in some areas and defeated in others. For instance, it is not difficult to find successful business people who have failed marriages.

For example, when you are enlightened about sound health, you will realize you are not meant to be sick. You will understand that your spirit is the real person, not your body. Your spirit has just been housed in the body. You will understand that when it seems like your body is out of balance or sick, it's like your phone's battery is dead. All you need to do is charge it, and everything will be fine. You will then understand why the Bible says, *"the spirit of a man will sustain him in sickness, but who can bear a broken spirit?"* (Proverbs 18:14). Even cancer can be destroyed when a person's spirit is enlightened or unbroken.

Being enlightened does not mean that you have knowledge of many things. The light comes when the truth dawns on you, and you commit yourself to practicing the truth you have received. I have had a few experiences of encountering light that has put me in command, by the grace of God.

Direct Light from the Word of God

I had a demonic encounter in my home country of Nigeria many years ago. I was on my way to visit a friend when a voodoo practitioner spat a strange substance into my eyes because I refused to be afraid of him like others were. From that moment on, I began to have trouble with my eyes. They ached badly from when I woke up to when I went to sleep. As a result of the eye pain, I would have to close my eyes for about an hour after reading for about fifteen to twenty minutes. It was a severe inconvenience. The ophthalmologists I visited in Nigeria and Poland told me that my eyes were reacting to unknown particles in the atmosphere. After struggling with that for many years, the siege was finally broken instantly after praying about it one day in my room. The pain in my eyes stopped, and I was healed.

It was not just the prayers that brought about the deliverance. It was prayers fuelled with faith. The faith arose when I got light from Deuteronomy 34:7, *"Moses was one hundred and twenty years old when he died. His eyes were not dim nor his natural vigor diminished."* I reasoned that if at age one hundred and twenty, Moses' eyes were still healthy, how come mine were having issues in my twenties? It was this light that empowered my simple prayer, and my healing came forth.

Indirect Light from the Word of God

There are times when you can access light from the words of anointed servants of God. Listening to anointed messages can allow us to receive a transfer of the light they carry in certain areas. I have had a few of those experiences.

I got light of my dominion over darkness while listening to a message by Dr. David Oyedepo. He was ministering on Colossians 2:15. While he was ministering, I saw what he was talking about. In that instance, I saw that Jesus had already disarmed all principalities and powers; hence, there was no reason to be afraid of a defeated foe. A few days later, as I was preparing to preach a message on Thanksgiving and was dancing in my room, my back became painfully stiff, and I could not stand upright. In a split second, though different thoughts of fear were racing through my mind, I immediately remembered Colossians 2:15 and ferociously declared, *"having disarmed principalities and powers, He made a public spectacle of them, triumphing over them in the cross; Satan, get your hands off my body now."* Immediately after I made this declaration, the pain disappeared, and I could stand upright again.

A few of my mentees have attested that they also experienced something similar. When it happened to them, they immediately remembered my testimony, started laughing spontaneously, and knocked out the devil just like I did. Praise the Lord!

The Bible tells us that the unfolding of God's word gives light (Psalms 119:130). Unfolding simply means when you understand the word. The unfolding can be done directly by the Holy Spirit or indirectly through anointed servants of God. When this light comes, you become enlightened and in command over the areas for which the light came.

When Understanding Comes, Light Comes

If using this means to enlightenment, there are a few things to note. The moment of enlightenment is the moment understanding comes.

The understanding I am referring to here is not your understanding. The Bible tells us not to lean on our own understanding. We have our human understanding and there is God's understanding. The Word of God says, *"Trust in the LORD with all your heart, And lean not on your own understanding"* (Proverbs 3:5). Human understanding is usually connected to our experiences and previous learnings. How many times have you felt that someone had something against you, only to find out later you were wrong? You probably thought that person had something against you because they ignored your greeting. God's understanding is trustworthy because He knows everything and can never be blindsided.

Human understanding is limited, while God's understanding is unlimited. God's understanding is unsearchable. *"Have you not known? Have you not heard? The everlasting God, the LORD, The Creator of the ends of the earth, Neither faints nor is weary. His understanding is unsearchable."* (Isaiah 40:28)

This clearly means that when we gain understanding of spiritual things, it is not because of our efforts; rather, it is because God gave us access to His understanding. How can you begin to search for something that is unsearchable? God gives us understanding, but we must desire to understand before its access can be granted to us.

"And we know that the Son of God has come and has given us an understanding, that we may know Him who is true; and we are in Him who is true, in His Son Jesus Christ. This is the true God and eternal life." (1 John 5:20)

When searching for understanding, do it with all your heart. Without a genuine heart, there will be no connection to God, the Father of lights.

"Pause and wonder! Blind yourselves and be blind! They are drunk, but not with wine; They stagger, but not with intoxicating drink. For the LORD has poured out on you The spirit of deep sleep, And has closed your eyes, namely, the prophets; And He has covered your heads, namely, the seers. The whole vision has become to you like the words of a book that is sealed, which men deliver to one who is literate, saying, "Read this, please." And he says, "I cannot, for it is sealed." Then the book is delivered to one who is illiterate, saying, "Read this, please." And he says, "I am not literate." Therefore the Lord said: "Inasmuch as these people draw near with their mouths And honor Me with their lips, But have removed their hearts far from Me, And their fear toward Me is taught by the commandment of men, Therefore, behold, I will again do a marvelous work Among this people, A marvelous work and a wonder; For the wisdom of their wise men shall perish, And the understanding of their pru-

dent men shall be hidden." Woe to those who seek deep to hide their counsel far from the LORD, And their works are in the dark; They say, "Who sees us?" and, "Who knows us?" Surely you have things turned around! Shall the potter be esteemed as the clay; For shall the thing made say of him who made it, "He did not make me"? Or shall the thing formed say of him who formed it, "He has no understanding?" (Isaiah 29:9-16)

God spoke through the Prophet Isaiah to the children of Israel and rebuked them for connecting to Him without their hearts. The repercussion of continuously offering lip service to God was that understanding was withdrawn from the people of Israel. God concealed knowledge from those who were typically known to be prudent. Note that God said, *"they removed their hearts from me."* Always be conscious of where your heart is and what it is focused on, especially when you're seeking God.

We are solely responsible for the state of our hearts. The people found themselves in a situation where they could no longer understand spiritual things, and *"therefore the Lord said "inasmuch as these people draw near with their mouths And honor Me with their lips, But have removed their hearts far from Me, And their fear toward Me is taught by the commandment of men, Therefore, behold, I will again do a marvelous work Among this people, A marvelous work and a wonder; For the wisdom of their wise men shall perish, And the understanding of their prudent men shall be hidden""* (Isaiah 29:13-14).

One way of knowing whether your heart is connected is to focus. Are you focusing on your quest to be enlightened in a particular area of life, or do you keep jumping from one quest to the other? Hear what the word of God says, *"When I applied my heart to know wisdom and to see the business that is done on earth, even though one sees no sleep day or night"* (Ecclesiastes 8:16). Without the genuine involvement of the heart, there will be no enlightenment.

We are also told to seek understanding like silver, and hidden treasures are sought. This means that our search for understanding should not be a passive endeavour. The advice from Solomon in Proverbs 2:2-6 is as follows, *"So that you incline your ear to wisdom, And apply your heart to understanding; Yes, if you cry out for discernment, And lift up your voice for understanding, If you seek her as silver, And search for her as for hidden treasures; Then you will understand the fear of the LORD, And find the knowledge of God. For the LORD gives wisdom; From His mouth come knowledge and understanding."*

God will never ask us to do what is impossible or to seek Him in vain. He wants us to find Him and the light that is ours as his children so we can demonstrate His nature on the earth.

Go searching for light and be willing to pay the price to get it. You will be happy that you did.

EVIDENCE OF UNDERSTANDING

Obedience

During one of our Bible studies at Cornerstone Christian Church of God, someone asked me a loaded question. She said, *"Is it possible to disobey even after you understand why God is asking you to do something?"* I said no, it's not possible. True understanding will lead to obedience.

Clarity of Speech

When you understand something, the way you communicate it will be simple. Out of the abundance of the heart, the mouth speaks (Matthew 12:34). If your heart understands, your communication will demonstrate it. You cannot give what you don't have.

Patience

A person with understanding is patient, because whoever is patient has great understanding (Proverbs 14:29). You can only display great patience, when you have enough understanding of why people do what they do. You are only able to display patience, when you understand the capability of the people you are asking do undertake certain tasks.

A person of understanding has a calm spirit (Proverbs 17:27). Knowledge is good, wisdom is better, and understanding is best. With understanding comes stability and depth. Understanding gives you an unrivalled calmness.

With knowledge, you can make others successful. With wisdom, you can become successful in some areas, but with understanding, you can replicate the success in every area of your life.

Boldness/Confidence

When you understand how something works, you are naturally confident. God has not given us the spirit of fear, but of power, love and a sound mind (2 Timothy 1:7). The sound mind in this passage is not just a mind that thinks but also one that understands.

In an interview with Bloomberg, Elon Musk said, *"When I was a little kid, I was really scared of the dark, but then I came to understand that dark just means the absence of photons in the visible wavelength (400 – 700 nanometers). Then I thought, it's really silly to be afraid of a lack of photons. Then I wasn't afraid of the dark after that."* This is just an example of how understanding can fuel confidence.

ENLIGHTENED OR WALKING IN THE LIGHT

There is a significant difference between being enlightened and walking in light.

Anybody can find light from the word of God concerning any area of their life. For instance, even unbelievers can have happy marriages if they find the truth from the Word of God and apply it. Anyone can prosper if they find the truth regarding lasting prosperity and commit to applying it.

The word of God is light. It can show you where you are going. You do not have to be enlightened to walk in the light of God's word.

When you are enlightened, you believe God's word, and become a carrier of light. An enlightened believer is the light.

However, only children of God can be enlightened by the light they receive. When we are enlightened, the light is not only on the outside but also inside. Only the children of God can be illuminated by the light they have received. The pure light of God cannot dwell in an impure heart.

A person walking in light can only find their way if they follow the light. An illuminated person, however, can provide light for others. This is similar to what the moon does; it reflects the light of the sun and can light up the sky at night.

When you are discussing with someone who is enlightened, you'll always seem to know what to do, and things become clear. That's because the light they carry is making it easy for you to see your way. If you discuss your issues with someone walking in light but not illuminated, most times, the best they can do is give you advice, which would be incomprehensible. An enlightened believer is meant to show others the way. An enlightened believer is the light of the world, a city set on a hill that cannot be hidden and is meant to use their light to direct others back to our loving Father in heaven (Matthew 5:14-16).

6

False Paths to Enlightenment

"The eyes of your understanding being enlightened; that you may know what is the hope of His calling, what are the riches of the glory of His inheritance in the saints." (Ephesians 1:18)

A human being can gain a semblance of enlightenment without being born again. That's why there are many so-called enlightened people in other religions. In the same way that the magicians also made their rods turn to snakes (Exodus 7:10-12), the devil can enable people to gain a semblance of enlightenment without Jesus Christ. Those people will also be able to perform miracles, speak deep words of wisdom, speak prophetic words, etc. There are many spirits out there that can enable anyone willing to pay the price to be enlightened, but the superior is Jesus Christ. God has given Him the name that is above every other name. Those enlightened through Jesus Christ will always triumph when engaged in one-on-one combat.

Being enlightened is more than experiencing a shiver. It is more than being able to bring about supernatural occurrences. It goes beyond being able to exercise higher levels of control over your mind, emotions, will and body.

With these other paths to enlightenment, you can gain command over the natural realm and your human senses, but these paths will not match up when faced with spiritual opposition.

These paths can give temporary control over the mind, emotions, will and body, but when it comes to the spiritual realm, the only authority higher than every other one is the authority in the name of Jesus Christ. The Word of God tells us that Jesus is head over all principalities and power (Colossians 2:10). Yes, some principalities can wield a certain amount of power here on earth. Yes, some powers can do superhuman things. The truth remains that Jesus has been given a name above every other name, and every other name will bow to the name of Jesus Christ (Philippians 2:9-11).

In the last days, it will be difficult to tell the difference between people who became enlightened through Jesus Christ and those who got enlightened through other false paths. The signs, wonders and miracles will look the same. There is one way that Jesus admonished us to differentiate those who are His from others. It is by the fruit that is produced. Do not make the mistake of using signs and wonders to tell the difference. Jesus specifically warned us in Matthew 7:13-20, *"Enter by the narrow gate; for wide is the gate and broad is the way that leads to destruction, and there are many who go in by it. Because narrow is the gate and difficult is the way which leads to life, and there are few who find it. "Beware of false prophets, who come to you in sheep's clothing, but inwardly they are ravenous wolves. You will know them by their fruits. Do men gather grapes from thorn bushes or figs from thistles? Even so, every good tree bears good fruit, but a bad tree bears bad fruit. A good tree cannot bear bad fruit, nor can a bad tree bear good fruit. Every tree that does not bear good fruit is cut down and thrown into the fire. Therefore by their fruits you will know them."*

Beware of false paths to receiving superhuman abilities. Beware of going through the broad gate to enlightenment and illumination. They may offer you a path to the same goals that I have mentioned in this book; however, if you follow those paths, the result will be destruction.

You may wonder, *"I have seen many of the spiritual leaders of those false paths, and they seem to bear good fruits."* That is why Jesus said you should be aware of wolves in sheep's clothing. Anyone or any path that does not take you back to your Heavenly Father through Jesus Christ is false and must be avoided.

Other paths to so-called enlightenment are hard drugs, asceticism (living a life of extreme discipline), yoga, extreme meditation, etc. All these will only offer temporary relief and "high," but the result has always been destruction.

Epilogue

You do not control when you will become enlightened. The Bible tells us in Ecclesiastes 9:11 that "... *the race is not to the swift, nor the battle to the strong, nor bread to the wise, nor riches to men of understanding, nor favor to men of skill; but time and chance happen to them all.*"

As you apply the principles from this book, engage your heart genuinely before God, but never allow haste or anxiety to take over. Impatience will give room for the devil to manipulate you. It will lead to errors. It could push you to look for faster and eventually destructive options.

God controls times and seasons. He knows when it is your time. A perfect mixture of your readiness and His timing will bring the light you need in every area of your life.

Patiently follow the steps outlined in this book, and you will shine like the stars. Let's light up the spiritual and earthly realm for Jesus Christ.

Contact the Author

I know without a doubt that this book has been a blessing to you. I am looking forward to hearing your testimony.

You can stay connected with me through the following platforms:

Instagram: e.adewusi | **Youtube:** Emmanuel Adewusi
Website: emmanueladewusi.org

Review the Book

A Sinner's Prayer

Dear Heavenly Father,

I come to You in the Name of Jesus Christ.

You said in Your Word, "Whosoever shall call upon the name of the Lord shall be saved." (Romans 10:13) I am calling on Your Name, so I know You have saved me now.

You also said that "if you confess with your mouth the Lord Jesus and believe in your heart that God has raised Him from the dead, you will be saved. For with the heart one believes unto righteousness, and with the mouth, confession is made unto salvation." (Romans 10:9-10) I believe in my heart Jesus Christ is the Son of God. I believe that He was raised from the dead for my justification, and I confess Him now as my Lord and Savior.

Thank you, Lord, because now, I am saved!

Thank You, Lord, because I know you have heard my prayer. Thank You, Lord, because I am now born again.

Signed _____

Date _____

About the Author

Apostle Emmanuel Adewusi is the Founding and Lead Pastor of Cornerstone Christian Church of God.

Called into ministry with the mandate to "bring restoration and transformation to all by teaching, preaching, and demonstrating the Gospel of Jesus Christ," he is passionate about seeing lives restored and transformed as God intended from the beginning of creation. He has a zeal for the full counsel of the Word of God, fellowship with the Holy Spirit, and being under spiritual authority.

He authored the books *"The Blessings of Being Under Spiritual Authority," "A Disciplined Life," "The Enlightened Believer," "The Skilled Sower,"* and other impactful titles. He has also released an album titled *"Divine Encounter"* and many more on the way.

Emmanuel Adewusi is joyfully married to his wife, Ibukun Adewusi, and together, they are building a thriving Christ-centered family.